PILGRIM'S REGRESS

PILGRIM'S REGRESS

GERMAN T. CRUZ

XULON PRESS

Xulon Press
2301 Lucien Way #415
Maitland, FL 32751
407.339.4217
www.xulonpress.com

Printed in the United States of America.

ISBN-13: 9781545616611

Acknowledgements

A LARGE EXPRESSION OF GRATITUDE IS extended to Fr. Peter B. Mangum, JCL, JV, Rector of the Cathedral of St. John Berchmans in Shreveport for his leadership and spiritual presence that motivated this culmination of a lifelong journey.

Deep appreciation is also expressed to Deacon John Basco, Director of Religious Education/RCIA for his indefatigable commitment to evangelism and teaching that served to guide the journey safely to its destination with great profit.

A vote of thanks is also extended to the entire team of RCIA for their commitment and gentility that made the journey more pleasant and inspiring.

Rev. Mgr. J. Carson La Caze, Parochial Vicar served as a great encourager and shepherd of the RCIA session group. To him we give praise and jubilation on his jubilee of priestly service.

Special note of admiration to my son Robert T. Cruz, Director of Music who has also directed our way on the path by example and work.

A deep expression of gratitude to the editorial team at Xulon Press who enhanced my manuscript and provided insightful analysis and spiritual encouragement.

Last but not least, loving thanks to Karen, my bride of 37 years who has walked many portions of this journey alongside me with enthusiasm and affection.

In the Manner of Introduction

FROM HISTORY AND LITERATURE WE KNOW somewhat well of John Bunyan's pilgrimage allegory (*A Pilgrim's Progress*, 1678) as a description of a journey of life by Christian from "this world to that which is to come" or simply from the City of Destruction to the Celestial City with myriad obstacles and temptations. Moreover, we are also aware of Dante Alighieri's tri-partite effort in *Divine Comedy* (1320) to amply illustrate contents and conditions of hell, purgatory and heaven as well as John Milton's ten books and over ten thousand lines of verse in *Paradise Lost* (1667). All three works sought to exhort readers in following a pathway of righteousness as a journey of life that culminates in a triumphal entry to the heavenly places. Above them stand the sacred words of *"Revelation"* with extensive and clear images of final judgment of evil and reward of good that are further emphasized elsewhere in Scripture by the statements of Jesus himself often presented in red letters that compel a life action centered upon obedience to His word and the guidance of the Holy Spirit. It all appears quite simple and direct when augmented with the many works of piety and discipline published over the past 1,000 years. There is no lack of advice or exhortation. The mechanics are well defined and tested. The road is well traced and the encouragement is generous. No reason for pilgrims to lose their way and lie disheartened by the roadside or obliterated on the travel lane as pieces of road kill. Yet, there is the ever-present issue of free will and the magnetic attraction of concupiscence in its widest expression beyond mere sexual context that distracts and detracts from good intentions. It is not merely physical or carnal desire that swallows us but it is also a highly toxic cultural force that pulls us down under the guise of intellectualism, progressivism and freedom or rights. The world is not permeated by the licentiousness of Las Vegas (What happens there stays there says the commercial) but there is a Las Vegas influence imbued in the world that sustains the overall culture in a very visible manner. We have grown accustomed to the presence of Las Vegas wherever we go. It is not a new thing since it dates from the farthest past as demonstrated by Sodom and the cities of the plain or the failings of King David. Nevertheless and probably more than at any other time, we are today seldom what we should be unless forcibly pushed inward to be. This is not just true of those who are alien to the Christian faith but also of those bred in it or wrapped in its influence. The normal has been altered and subsumes both the faithful and the pagan into spiritual and cultural black holes that are accepted as destinations of substance.

The pursuit of righteousness is exhausting and befuddling for most pursuers and backsliding becomes more than a winter Olympic sport. Many exhausted pilgrims lay by the side of the road meekly raising their arms in search of help like victims of a great tsunami. For each person avoiding the grafting into the rootstock of faith there is also someone trying to return to the stock seeking to be re-grafted or fertilized for new growth taken by a desire for regress along with a feeling of regret. It is essentially an effort to center or find order after the exhaustion of the searching journey. The regret is framed in the awareness of having missed something of value mixed with the anxiety of recovering it or acquiring it fresh. This book will seek to describe one such return or redress in the hope of encouraging others who are wandering far from the rooting stock to find a way back to what once nurtured them. It is an effort to purposely renew the flow of divine sap that nurtures the spirit. The stock might still hold them but the sap is not flowing fast and plentiful enough to promote great growth and fruitful production. More than a manual of devotions and procedures, this book will attempt to present a life context of seeking and returning that could be useful to promote or stimulate a journey of return rather than a mere exercise in commiseration.

On a scholarly note for the sake of establishing a clear definition let us understand that the title comes from Latin *regressus*, derived from *regredi* 'go back, return' . This selection reflects the fact that there was not a radical departure but rather a drifting away and a journey of re-encounter. It is well advised to dig into the basic root of words to enunciate a correct meaning that can provide guidance and clarity. Knowing origins can assist on the understanding of destinations. By vocational influence I write in brush strokes derived from my plastic arts background. The page is for me a canvas for watercolors and color pencils augmented by metaphoric expressions derived from my poetic affinities. This book is not a formal academic essay but rather a *'cri de coeur'* (cry from the heart) that flows from my most intimate regions with the intention of showing the merciful touch of Christ in my life.

One: A Proper Foundation

FIRST, IT IS NECESSARY TO KNOW BEGINNINGS, to understand bases and places, to know first steps. I was born of a young couple married in the Roman Catholic Church almost 20 years before Vatican II. Dedicated through baptism on the 8th day after birth. Named after a beloved grandfather and given a middle name in homage to St. Jude Thaddaeus as a special devotion of the mother. Joining a long line of grandparents and relatives sustained in the Roman Catholic faith with a life heritage that could be traced to family origins in northern and western Spain. Educated in public schools with strong Christian catechesis leading to first communion and confirmation before middle school. Instructed in liturgical Latin as altar boy helping not only with masses but also packing and distributing food for the poor in the parish pantry. By all estimates expected to become a priest. Charged with living a holy life while having the heart tugged by the increasing evidence of poverty all around the city. How to help beyond the weekly and ineffective food distribution? How to bring hope in the midst of despair? Was there a way beyond the sermons and scarcity of donations? How to bridge the class and race differences? These questions in various modalities have framed my entire life.

Despite all the efforts at piety in bliss, there was in me an increasing burden of concern for the poor. Poverty appeared immune to prayer and

1

good wishes. In my mind I could see that Jesus fed multitudes but we were unable to feed a dozen. The supplications and concern were easy to muster but the response in provision for effective solutions was absent. What was wrong? There was a lack of sufficiency in all. It was as if the daily bread provided in response to prayer was kept hidden by those to whom the provision had been entrusted for sharing with the least of all. Crossing social and cultural fences in a very stratified society began to appear as an almost impossible task unmoved by pious postures and pleadings. Was there another option beyond hearty Ave Maria proclamations and exercises in personal good intentions? Where was the power promised in the gospels? How much faith and supplications was necessary to feed and clothe the poor? Did not Jesus promise that all our requests would be satisfied? Was there something lost in the translation?

At my confirmation I was given a copy of the *"Spiritual Exercises of St. Ignatius of Loyola"* along with a volume of *"The Imitation of Christ"*. On its purest form they were nice gift leather bound volumes with gilded edges and my name engraved on the cover. Beyond that there was an implied wish for the pursuit of holiness with a tangential calling to vocational commitment. Somehow Loyola, Kempis and the gift giver expected a commitment I was not yet ready to give or understand. Perhaps I was not yet saintly enough despite my altar boy and charity activity. Perhaps I lacked sufficient vocation or vision or faith and it was noticeable. How to be saintly, pious, holy and compassionate in the midst of so much misery? I could not adopt then the "indifference" called for by Loyola despite the four week effort of the spiritual exercises during Lent that were intended to lead me into righteousness or a closer relation to God. Imitation as posited by Kempis demanded far too much sacrifice in my pre-teen years loaded with illusions of great athletic and academic performances.

Our usual teachers of catechism were Franciscans that emphasized humility and peacemaking contrary to our juvenile search for interpersonal conflict. During Lent they were replaced by a group of Jesuits that would lead us for four weeks in spiritual exercises. This was a much welcome period by the faculty because of the enforced change in our conduct. It did not transform the school into a quiet monastery but it came close as we walked in the awareness of our wretchedness constantly preached from the pulpit. The Jesuits saw fit to convict us of sin and they succeeded beyond expectations. I did not realized how much sin I was already carrying in my early years.

With my leather bound copy of the *"Exercises"* I marched with classmates into the school chapel to start the first week of something we barely understood but all feared. Jesuits in black cassocks project a formidable force and the dialectical exhortation to repentance was merciless. From the onset during the *"examen"* or examination of conscience we were directed to pray for God's presence in our lives followed by several steps of gratitude, self-assessment of daily life, repentance for sin, and request for sufficient grace to engage the challenges of the next day. We could easily feel the heat of the flames of hell. In a couple of weeks we were introduced to something called "prayer of contemplation" that was vastly different from our various memorized prayers. It was supposed to be a focused meditation upon a Bible passage with the basic problem that we had been instructed in catechism for six years but had not been taught reading of the Bible or even page through it. Our theological knowledge was based on soft stories from biblical characters and brief homiletic references at mass rather than a direct reading of Scripture. From *Genesis* to *Revelation* the big book was a foreboding dimension we were careful not to enter. The overall view in the community was that our minds were ill prepared to deal with the power of Scripture. Only the priests and some well learned individuals were able to decipher its message and understand its meaning. We did the best we could handling the small Bibles from the back of the pews and rejoiced after the closing mass right before Palm Sunday and a Holy Week vacation time. The spiritual exercises were finished and would not occur for another year. In all, Loyola affected my early teens with questions about faith and salvation that lasted most of my life. There was in them a demand for discipline and direction along with zeal and commitment. I needed it all but to know and to do are two different verbs rarely convergent. Many questions kept coming to the fore then as always. Was my salvation more important than that of those around me in light of the "indifference" urged by Loyola toward the created things? Was salvation restricted to some group alone? Was it reserved for only those committed to priestly or cloistered lives? I could see how life in a cloister could promote virtue but also how it could encourage a distancing from the reality of humanity. Praying the *Liturgy of the Hours* every day sounded fine but there was a need for time to be invested in other more human pursuits. It seemed then to me that I needed to be in the world but not of the world as Jesus interceded (John 17:16-17) in his prayer. Holiness could be pursued away from cloisters and orders. The pursuit would then be about an enduring relationship with God rather than merely to a cloistered state. Being drafted into an army would not make you more of a warrior than feathers on wax wings can make you into a bird as Icarus found out to his peril. The exercises pulled me in one direction while events around me demanded some direct action in another that was spiritual in part. The gift of the leather bound *"Exercises"* spoke of someone's desire for my spiritual journey but my mind and will spoke of a different path not less holy. Could there be holiness outside or parallel to the church? Life was sure to provide an answer.

The voices from the pulpit and the public plaza spoke with eloquence of untenable and ideal solutions far removed from the daily reality. Many promises were made into the air above the multitudes. Oratorical skill was tantamount to great intellectual acuity. People loved to hear words flowing like music with little consequence. The Word made flesh had power but the fleshy words of men were sterile despite their apparent eloquence. I listened with question marks popping into my head like shots from a machine gun. Questions rose demanding answers more than rhetorical contentment. How long should a poor man wait for a morsel? There was food at the Sermon of the Mount. There was salvation at Golgotha. There was nothing but crushed hope at the plaza and the pulpit. It all came to the issue of whether poverty was a form of earthly purgatory? How could one be holy in a deprived and aggrieved environment? The voices within me jeered at my confusion and frustration like geese attacking a cornfield. Voices echoing in my heart and mind that seemed to vanish in the prayer space between my knees and eternity. Perhaps none of my prayers could reach beyond the ceiling of my room or the apse at the cathedral. I felt utterly useless and powerless. Much like a man trapped in an invisible impenetrable box just like a mime or possibly a mummy.

Certainly, it was not that I did not know about charity in both the sense to love and to give. Examples of charity abounded around me. At home my mother fed whoever came and handed food and our old clothes to those who needed them. She was not so much a saint but a compassionate person trying to help the less fortunate and the ignorant. Sainthood was not her sole pursuit since service was her constant calling. She did not pray constantly or go to church assiduously. Raising seven children while running a farm can take some time out of the daily devotional routine. Her love was expressed in giving and comforting with joy.

It was not a great effort by the overwhelming larger dimension of the need. Yet it was something concrete and palpable. We were neither poor nor rich but we were taught from the earliest age to be kind and generous with all people and with our gifts. To practice devotion, humility and holiness at the pew as well as in the street. Ignatius of Loyola might have liked her. In complement, my grandmother spent ample time in her kneeling bench each day despite her advancing age and struggle with advancing Alzheimer's praying for the intercession and blessing of several saints, reciting the rosary and receiving communion once a week from a visiting Eucharistic outreach of the parish. Somehow there seemed to be no evident response to her prayers other than the comfort of her intercession. She died one afternoon coiled in her bed probably waiting for answers. I prayed also with less fervor than her but equal expectancy for what I probably did not understand fully despite the explicit promise in the gospel that whatever we needed (John 15:7) and would be given to us. Most certainly, this passage has been interpreted many ways by many people in contrary denotations and theological arguments with a veneer of authority. I have chosen to ignore the interpretations except for what the passage says both in English and Greek trying to understand and expect nothing more. If this promise was subject to a larger explanation, it belies other promises upon which we base our faith. Jesus did not speak with footnotes or amplified scholarly annotations that merited great review and commentary. His word is truth and nothing else. Just like on the first day of creation. Nevertheless, when you ask and do not receive, you are probably found unworthy of your petition and it is best to go on to another plan.

By any measure, my petitions were insufficiently supported by abject need or so I thought. Despite all, poverty was not only evident but also quite troubling all around me. What could a child do? This is the beginning of my first great spiritual crisis. I had encountered a rather harsh recognition of limitations and meanings in the practical application of faith. It was possible that my value and power as an intercessor and interpreter was negligible. I probably lacked the true anointing or at least was ignorant of the proper liturgical formulas. He who has nothing must do something with the nothing he has been given. So, I continued on my journey with the suspicion that there was a large chasm between wishing and receiving.

As I moved from elementary to middle school and then on to high school I began to become aware through readings and conversations of themes in Liberation Theology[1] and Marxism that presented apparently well articulated solutions to the social issues that were source of my frustrations. Issues articulated in books and essays rather than merely voiced in public plazas and pulpits. Issues that apparently had no need of additional divine intervention and demanded human action in faith as confirmation of their provenance. God had spoken and all that remained was the execution of His word. It was all very simple. The notions of social and political revolution led by men to create a just order began to fill my mind to nurture a fresh hope of revolutionary change. Living in a Catholic country dedicated to the Sacred Heart of Jesus with its periodic celebrations of holy feast days provided neither evidence of action nor effective sympathy for the plight of the poor. It all seemed reduced to oratory and little action that was probably affirmed in the gospel assurance that the poor will always be with us. Nevertheless it was apparent that our quota of poor people and their misery was quite large. Both the needs and the people were real rather than mere figures of speech or

---

[1] Gutierrez, Gustavo. *Teología de la Liberación, Perspectivas.* Centro de Estudios y Publicaciones, Lima, 1971 Jose Miguez-Bonino. *¿Qué significa ser iglesia de Cristo aquí, hoy?* Methopress, Buenos Aires, 1966

subjects for dissertations. Thus, José Miguez-Bonino, Gustavo Gutierrez and the Boff brothers (Leonardo and Clodovis) made sense to me as I navigated my faith in high school through elements of Liberation Theology buffeted by the usual Marxist influences dressed as liberalism and progressivism. It appeared as if a radical and rapid solution was emerging on the horizon to the problems of poverty and other social ills. There was a ferment of hope on the horizon. It then occurred to me that in some way the Ascension had left the church bereft of creativity by the removal of the Creator despite the awesome miracle of Pentecost some 1900 years in the past. Creativity is then to be considered as the filling of the Holy Spirit to move the faithful into action. It is not a calling to passivity or timorous whining. In this sense, creativity is the full face of truth. The Creator had been removed in favor of the bureaucracy and in so doing we negate the power of the Spirit to be replaced by fear of doing God's will. This has been one of the preferred standard procedures in the full extent of Christianity for two thousand years. Today, more than ever, we needed the full divine presence (power)[2] with a strong creative voice rather than cadres of chief operating officers and liturgical planners busily filling forms and arranging events. Creativity fosters courage and courage feeds action. It was so in the first century and so it could be twenty centuries later. Pentecost was not a typical office staff meeting but rather a divine driven ordination into power. The apostles and the saints have given testimony of this. What we celebrate most in them is their courage to be faithful on the face of evil. The power of the Spirit enabled the power of their deeds. A power that came with no expiration

---

[2] The promise was fulfilled at Pentecost and the charge was that with the Spirit the church could be a transformational power in the world. The Spirit being the essence of the Creator imbued with power moving mortals to be creative *"But ye shall receive power, after that the Holy Ghost is come upon you: and ye shall be witnesses unto me both in Jerusalem, and in all Judaea, and in Samaria, and unto the uttermost part of the earth"*. Acts 1:8 KJV

date or need of recharge. I found myself becoming more spiritual but less "religious" as Loyola would see me. His six paths to God[3] merged with various emphases upon my own path.

I could well imagine the crucified Jesus that I saw captured in the altars surrounded by votive candles now descending with power to lead His people in the healing of all things. The groans of creation were seeking the mercy of the Creator through his empowered people. Dialectically, this had to happen. It could not be otherwise. This was no mere Pentecostal wish fulfillment clouded by the fog of our timidity. Jesus presence was not a concept in clouds of incense but a reality that needed to emerge from the dust of poor neighborhoods. It says toward the end of *Revelation* (21:5) that the one seated in the throne says: *"Behold, I make all things new."* This might be taken to mean that the current conditions will persist for a long time into eternity or until He comes again (even at this moment). From Pentecost we are his duly empowered agents and the need can be addressed with our faithful exercise of courage nourished by His Spirit. The need for justice and provision was urgent. It was something for now rather than the hereafter.

The reality of poverty demanded urgency. A timid church could not answer the call of the gospel. Submission to Christ was meant as a call to courage rather than to a hiding place behind the reredos. In submission we inherited the courage of Christ walking up to Golgotha along with the power of Pentecost to spur the church into action. Although there can be found in *Revelation* an exegetical justification for meekness given our weak human and sinful condition there is always the call to

---

[3] The six paths, identified by Father James Martin, SJ in *The Jesuit Guide to Almost Everything: A Spirituality for Real Life*. Harper One. New York. 2012 are: Belief, Independence, Disbelief, Return, Exploration, and Confusion. They serve to define my search across my lifetime with greater emphasis upon a few. Others have done similar observations like Merton in an effort to provide an analysis of spiritual pilgrimages in search for God.

overcome just as Jesus himself as recorded in his triumphal boast (John 16:33) Of course, people with a better knowledge of theology certainly knew better or were expected to do so. The capacity of discernment by the entire magisterium of the church corporation could be contrasted with the uneducated understanding of a young high school well-wisher. What could such a young man do? The urgency and the need would continue unabated despite theological disquisitions.

Pope Leo XIII was deeply moved by the conditions of work and poverty in the world that led him to write 86 encyclicals intended to do much to arouse the conscience of Catholics and the world but they are forgotten and rest now only as subjects of curatorial processes. In my case, *Rerum Novarum* (1891) served almost seventy years later as a strong immunization shot against the fantasy of Marxism and an affirmation of the possibilities of the New Kingdom under Christ. These encyclicals are often treated as words from another time much in the manner we treat Scripture. Yet, they have enduring effect. For this effort alone Leo XIII should have been canonized and declared a Doctor of the Church. None of this will ever happen because. . . . because. . . .Because: The poor we shall always have with us and no more excuses are necessary. The procedures and liturgies are all well set.

As part of the Christianity teaching component of the high school curriculum a Dominican priest taught us philosophy and patristic history. He listened patiently to my harangues and questions with encouragement to study further beyond high school and the moment. He recognized a quality in me that had remained hidden under the academic activity and my political pursuits. He had given us an IQ test and afterwards began to express higher expectations of several of my classmates commensurate with the scores. We had to live up to our potential by pursuing more education in order to be more charitable with our gifts.

He argued that talent lay in deposit within us and we had to increase its value. The possibility of attending college was quite far removed from my reach since my family had no great means for such effort and we were seven children. Nonetheless, my parents and grandparents supported my ambition placing hope in Divine Providence. I held firmly to my Miraculous Medal with all the faith I could muster and much to my surprise I was awarded a full scholarship to study abroad after excelling in some academic tests. Somehow the prayers of many had been answered or were they remnants from those of previous generations that had gone unanswered in some overloaded heavenly mailbox? The award left me very happy but also conflicted about abandoning the theater of political and faith action that was giving me a protagonist role. How could I leave the familiar confines of the home field for places yet unknown at the moment when my social and spiritual consciousness was taking shape? The Dominican referred me to the already familiar passage in Mathew 26:11 where Jesus affirms the constant presence of the poor suggesting that they would be there upon my return and that I would also find more poor people wherever I went. Above all he insisted upon me to continue my spiritual journey focusing on Christ and a possible encounter with Him. By reason of the answered prayer I had been anointed with a high expectation that now had to be fulfilled. Encountering Christ would now become the focus of my journey. Merely knowing that the poor existed was not a solution but rather a beginning point.

Two: A Relocated Soul

DISTANCE OFFERS A FRESH PERSPECTIVE OR AT least a change of vanishing points. A distance of 2,600 miles in a new environment serves to promote several changes of location, culture and attitude. The largest issue rested on survival expectations within a very large academic institution where only 25% of the freshman class would graduate in four years. On top of that was the issue of keeping the scholarship with a sufficient satisfactory grade point average. My capacity and capability would be challenged like never before far away from the familiar. Negative expressions and questions of failure abounded. Fortunately, my academic advisor was wise beyond my expectations and led me away from the dumbed down classes for foreign students that offered no credit of significance but demanded as much time as those in the regular curriculum. He considered that I was not to think of myself as a foreign student but rather a capable student born elsewhere. Being admitted at this university had some meaning after all. The advisor trusted my capacity for performance and signed me up for classes without consideration to my status. Initially, I was apprehensive but not fearful. My language comprehension scores were quite high and once in the classroom I would be able to behave unlike a "foreign" student in need of some coddling. Thus, I stayed away from the entire apparatus of care for foreign students that somehow appeared to me as an expression of concern for a handicapped sector with a dollop of sympathy. I was going to succeed or fail on my own effort with no concessions. Jesus had called the paralytic to abandon his cot and walk (John 5:8) just as I was challenged to engage without excuses. The miracle resided not merely in the award of scholarship but it had a lasting effect of subsequent performance

To my surprise, I made the dean's list on 7 out of 8 semesters and three summer sessions. The one semester I missed the list I was fighting a debilitating cold like affliction (aka pneumonia), a harsh winter and some depression triggered by the loneliness that often strikes people removed from the familiar. Swimming in a heavy current presents very clear options between drowning outright and floating to shore despite swallowing some water in the process. My spirits were low at that time but the rigorous demands of academic work kept me above water. Carrying a big load of credit hours per semester was a hard undertaking but everybody around me was doing it and I could do no less. It was possible that I missed my home environment and was not really fully acclimated to my new place and pursuit. Assimilation carries the critical moment of disconnection and re-engagement just like in the plugging and unplugging of a lamp. My life of social involvement was now refocusing on academic pursuits and an independent lifestyle away from the once normal. School, parish and family were now points on the horizon. Retrospectively, I can say that my soul was adrift despite my academic success and this could have been the cause of my distress. In the distancing from my home I began to explore ways to kindle my spiritual journey. Popular rock-and-roll music began to provide some joyful context while also indulging on an exploration of Zen Buddhism via D. T. Suzuki's *"Introduction to Zen Buddhism"* and Alan Watts's *"The Way of Zen"*. This led me eventually to a reading of *"The Seven Storey Mountain"* by Thomas Merton that created in me an urge for the contemplative life in retreat further animated by his *"Thoughts in Solitude".* Somehow I began to think that conflicts of life and faith could be resolved by a cloistered life. I needed to break away from the world and embrace solitude and silence like Merton had done except that I was no Merton.

Somehow the influence of Loyola from those periods of spiritual exercise faded behind the literary power of Merton and new experiences. Merton and the Beatles co-existed in my mind with concurrent efforts to engage Zen. All was possible in the realm of imagination and desire with no need for rationality. During the summer of the *"Sargent Pepper"* (1967) album before the release of *"All You Need is Love"* as a single recording, my spirit had found some contentment greatly amplified by a desire to explore Merton's universe as if it were a destination in outer space. At that point all was magical just like the Beatles album *"The Magical Mystery Tour"* (1967) after which I wanted much more to travel to the Abbey in Gethsemani to see what life was like in the monastery where Merton lived. His death (1968) augmented in me the desire to know more and possibly follow in his footsteps. Not so much that I would be an heir but rather another writer and student in a journey of the spirit in a quieter environment. In my mind, I considered myself a good candidate for the monastery. My spiritual pathway seemed to converge toward a reclusive life. So, I read about the rule of Saint Benedict, the order of La Trappe and the procedures for admission. Much to my chagrin, the admission into the monastic life was a rather lengthy process involving preliminary psychological testing, some time as a postulant and a few years as a novice before being found competent to be accepted and eventually taking the final vows to become a "fully professed" monk. The Abbey at Gethsemani was not like the French Foreign Legion. Intelligence and creativity were not solely the attributes that the trappists were looking for or it could be that they were not what I was looking for once the consequences were revealed. In all, Gethsemani was filled with silence and hard work within the *Liturgy of the Hours* and Gregorian chanting. I could not bring along my worldly luggage complete with albums and books into a small contemplative cell. The Beatles and much less the Rolling Stones or even Steppenwolf did not fit. Entering the monastery was very much like the entrance of Saint Francis to the church in Assisi by divesting himself totally of all possessions even his clothes. The freedom I had perceived and admired in Merton was not immediately available to somebody still ambivalent as to a place to belong. Merton had been a special case and I was not quite so special. Obviously I was not ready to abandon the world as such and I preferred then to pursue contemplation by other means that did not preclude social action. For some reason I was a man of action seeking fast solutions to what increasingly appeared to be slow moving problems and possibilities. The voice of Horace inherited from Hippocrates came then to mind: *"Ars longa, vita brevis, occasio praeceps, experimentum periculosum, iudicium difficile." Art is long but life is brief, opportunity fleeting, experiment treacherous, judgement difficult"* Perhaps I was a mere spiritual dabbler rather than a committed faith practitioner and truth seeker. Could there be time for centering over a long life? Was I a hummingbird rather than an eagle drifting majestically rather than a small shiny bird impatiently pecking flowers for a brief taste of nectar?

Inevitably, college graduation came and with it the need to seek a life outside the academic safe spaces. Just like the sentiments before leaving home, the departure from the university was fraught with anxieties related as before to my capacity to succeed and survive in new environments for which I was supposed to have been prepared. Periodic meditation brought some level of calm but a consistent discipline seemed to evade my best intentions. Somehow, Merton still made sense and served as a guide despite my spiritual journey away from the original faith. I read most of his works on contemplation seeking some sort of spiritual axis. With time my capacity for meditation improved significantly along with a sharper perception that was very useful in my design discipline. I could see better both physically and mentally.

In the midst of the college years I met a very intelligent young woman that captivated all my senses. As it goes in Johnny Cash's "Jackson" we "got married in a fever, hotter than a pepper sprout" and set out to conquer the big city after graduation. A college classmate guide me to a good job and many good times followed until the fire began to go our after a few years. My daughter arrived and soon thereafter the marriage began to unravel. Intent on saving it by any means, I accepted a position at a firm in another state, bought a house and made plans for relocating after extensive discussion with wife and friends. Sadly, this was not the solution to the marital strife and soon my wife demanded a divorce taking custody of my daughter and forcing the quick sale of the new house at a significant loss. With a floating rate mortgage at a high interest point I had to bring in money at closing and pay up some perceived equity from the shared down payment we had made at purchase time for the house. A second great spiritual crisis enveloped me and I left my new job dejected and bankrupt seeking some consolation in the work of Boethius (*The Consolation of Philosophy*). His old (AD 524) but classic argument for the transitory nature of fame and wealth along with the superiority of things of the mind and the supremacy of happiness that comes from within spoke rather eloquently to me and enabled a long and painful period of recuperation. I had not failed before and these hard fallings had shaken my entire being. How could I get up to engage life again? A full eclipse had come over me and dark hours of the soul hounded me for almost one year. My whole life had crashed and for the first time I had neither hope nor desire. Meditation and contemplation were futile. My mind could not focus and my spirit lay in tatters. Unlike Boethius I was not executed although my entire being was in a coma.

Again, a college friend came to my rescue with a kind and generous offer of temporary housing and guidance to a part-time teaching job at the local university. My value was slowly restored and a promising new job in another region soon emerged. I felt then like a mummy ripping the burial wrappings or even like a larva breaking out of the pupa to become a butterfly. Life was beginning to be joyful and hopeful once again. Zen was in the trash and rock-and-roll had given way to Bach and baroque.

Three: A New Landscape

BEFORE MOVING TO THE NEW JOB I MARRIED A
gentle and beautiful woman I had come to know during my teaching
sojourn. It was mostly her gentleness that prompted my healing and
moved my heart. With her a new journey began with increasing vigor.
The new location and work calling brought great excitement to my life
and a renewed longing for a spiritual connection began to flutter again
in my heart. All the new goodness was not of my own making. I was
convinced then that somehow forces beyond my control were operating
for my good. My work provided extensive practice in community design
that expanded both my knowledge and vocational aptitudes. In order
to round up my skills I studied business management and development
feasibility that soon became cornerstones of my professional service. A
time in the desert was now being replaced by a fresh start in a new place.

To the challenge of work and family was added an invitation by a
co-worker to attend church. After 12 years of absence, I went to a sanctuary with no knowledge of denominational purposes or creedal state-
ment. It was not a Roman Catholic Church but rather an independent
dispensationalist community congregation that welcomed us with effu-
sion and kindness. The spiritual journey had begun anew. An elderly
pastor took me under his wing as a disciple. Every Thursday for about
one year I met with him after work for counseling and conversation. He

was quite serious about memorization of Scripture as a healing agent for the soul in a manner that was not very much different from my previous Zen koan exercises. He gave me an initial list of 10 verses that I memorized while driving in a 45-minute commute to and from work. I soon began to notice a pleasant change in mind and heart. It was sort of a peaceful feeling of order and purpose. After mastering the ten verses he encouraged me to go a bit further and memorize longer passages with the ultimate goal of committing an entire book to memory. It was very much in the fashion of the dystopian science fiction story *Fahrenheit 451* by Brad Bradbury directed for film by François Truffaut with Oskar Werner, Cyril Cusak and Julie Christie in the main roles. Fahrenheit 451 is the temperature at which paper burns. The story presents the effort by an oppressive future government to eliminate all literature by means of a force known as the Firemen charged to seek and set ablaze any and all books. A fireman is asked by a school teacher if he reads the books he is burning and causes him out of curiosity to begin reading a few. Eventually he confronts a book collector that argues about the power of books to change lives and exposes him to the group known as the "book people" that has memorized books in order to keep them alive. The fireman eventually decides to join the "book people" and selects a work by Edgar Allan Poe to memorize. Without thinking it twice, I took to the challenge of memorizing an entire book. Perhaps memorization of Scripture has a dual value of preserving it and preserving us in the increasingly oppressive environment that seeks to limit and extinguish the Christian faith.

So, I memorized *Philippians* over one month of commuting and was called by the old pastor to recite it as a homily during an evening service that resulted in encouragement for others to take on similar challenges. To them I was a stranger from the Third World with a bit of an accent.

The old pastor re-qualified me as a gift from another world. I felt very blessed. Next I tackled *Ephesians* right before the birth of my son who now carries the name of this pastor as a living tribute to someone who shed light on my pathway to truth. A man much like Melchizedek who was able to reach deep within my spirit to bring about peace and joy that enabled a better view of the supernatural in light of the merely natural. Words in memory seem to establish order and guide life by their constant presence. Memory cannot be put in the bookshelf for later review when it might be convenient. The impact is both immediate and constant.

Like all pilgrims whether by faith or vocation, my skills could not remain in one place and I was eventually promoted to a branch in a larger city with greater (probably more daunting) responsibilities. Again, the conflict of departure arose although they were greatly mitigated by a renewed faith and the confidence it had given me. The experiences acquired and developed in my work began to prove worthwhile in my lifelong quest for improvement in the lives of the poor. It seems as if I was being prepared for action further down the road. The maker of the universe could watch over me anywhere in his creation. Scripture kept in my mind kept flashing upon my pathway. My pilgrimage has acquired renewed focus. The new location would bring about a test of acuity in both spirit and mind. I was reaching a fruiting stage with some trepidation and much expectation. What would the fruit be?

four: A few Pathway Interchanges

THE NEW CITY OFFERED MANY PROFESSIONAL
and spiritual challenges and opportunities. My skills were honed for
extensive utilization to promote exciting outcomes. I was maturing as
a professional and had a clearer vision of my journey of faith. After a
considered (say agonizing) search we joined a Southern Baptist church
near our home. It was a large place that welcomed us with a continuation of study of Scripture, volunteering, using vocational skills and
even taking a few early steps into teaching. Some wonderful friend-
ships were developed along personal and faith lines. It seemed as if all
of life was converging toward a higher and larger purpose. My classmate
friend of a previous black night of the soul returned from a sojourn in
Australia and encouraged me to start my own studio as an expression
of confidence on skills and faith. It was a daunting suggestion since I
had never been on my own as a practicing professional. How would I
run a business? Could I survive the pressures of work and family that
would ensue? How to do marketing and produce outcomes? The questions kept popping into my fearful mind not unlike fireworks. A few
long days of hard thinking and searching for calm followed. I sought
advice from a few friends and some clients while also delving into some
contemplative prayer as I had learned in high school. This was truly

a great challenge quite different from any I had encountered before. There was a consensus that affirmed the capacity of my talent far above what I thought of myself. The moment was ripe and I went out on my own working from my garage. Several previous clients lent me support with work contracts after they had fulfilled the engagements with my previous employer. New friends came to the fore with words of encouragement and leads to work opportunities. It was a rather wonderful situation made easier by the assurance of Scripture. Truly, I did not know how good I was at my discipline not for reason of humility but simply because I was always concentrated on doing my best without looking back or seeking praise. That was what I had been instructed to do in college and what my time of contemplation had shaped my mind and heart to be. You deliver your all and your best as a matter of doing what is expected. Nothing more, nothing less. It was all a wonderful situation. My young son could visit my office often and I could work at any time and have time to do things with family. Providentially, income flow did not change and a few expenses actually diminished. A good friend from church volunteered to act as my lawyer, adviser and encourager affirming a spiritual bond that made it all possible and pleasant. My faith acquired a stronger context in a blending with life. A clear path for the journey had begun to emerge.

A challenge to use my gifts for the benefit of others soon came. A historical black community on the edge of the central city wanted to articulate a plan for renovation and preservation. They had no means to hire a professional and several faithful people with a missionary impetus called on me to volunteer my services. Working alone offered me a lot of flexibility in time and resource allocation. After some introductions and conversations, a linkage was established to provide services on a pro-bono fashion. Thus started a six year pro-bono engagement that extended from the production of a simple conceptual development plan to the implementation of measures of preservation, rehabilitation and new construction that enveloped residences, businesses and schools in a 20 block neighborhood. This was how the development of skills, mind and heart across college and professional practice had come to bear fruit. Before I could see it, God had it prepared for me at this time. Now I had both a business and a missionary task fully consecrated to the will of God and stretching my stamina and capacity. To make things more complicated I entered a Southern Baptist theological seminary to pursue a Master of Divinity as a means to articulate my faith action with greater authority. At this point I felt very much like the daredevil trying to jump several cars while doing a forward flip. What was the worst that could happen?

My professional experience and skills enabled a comprehensive response to needs and my spiritual context provided depth to my insight. The material and the spiritual were coming together to rehabilitate what was considered lost or unfit. Echoes of Nehemiah ran often through my mind as I contemplated the physical condition of the neighborhood. The spiritual aspect was addressed sufficiently by several elderly and dedicated pastors of small churches. There was faith in abundance that gave inevitability to the redevelopment effort. Somehow, all things ran smoothly until the neighborhood fell under the sphere of influence of planning for the Olympic games. It had been decided that the Olympic Stadium would be located in a corner of the neighborhood with a corresponding demand for parking space that could bring about the demolition of several residential blocks. How much should a community give away to support a big event of negligible impact? The entire process of revitalization already on the way could be radically interrupted to the detriment of the neighborhood. To say that the challenge acquired

Olympic dimensions is to say very little. The simple suddenly became complex and the peaceful became rapidly urgent and often irritating. Voices from all types of persuasions were now clamoring for attention and influence. A more detailed plan emerged with clear objectives to preserve the outer skin of the community and promote some new residential construction to sustain community vitality. It was now necessary to find new alliances and supporters to safeguard the integrity of the neighborhood plan. Quite surprisingly, support came from many sources and the energy of the upcoming event helped propel the achievement of plans for rehabilitation of existing housing and the construction of new homes. Several programs for improvement of schools and public housing also surfaced and a new athletic warm up center was built in the core of the neighborhood on what once had been a sanitary landfill. The effort of a six-year labor was producing an unexpected harvest of good fruits. The neighborhood would not become a parking lot after all.

In the process of getting acquainted with needs and wants of the neighborhood I visited several homes and talked with many people. Various levels of poverty became evident along with individual efforts to change life stations. Many expressions of gratitude or interest were offered with curiosity as to my intentions and capabilities. There was little talk of race and much discussion over liberation from poverty and aspirations for the children. One vent in particular served to emphasize upon me the nature and extent of the effort. I visited an apartment in the public housing component of the community and found a young mother with two children living in total darkness. She asked if I could bring some candles and I inquired as to the condition of the electrical service. Her lights had been out for several weeks and no maintenance workers had yet responded to her call for help. I unscrewed a light bulb and found out it was burnt out. Saying little I went to the market and purchased several bulbs to install upon my return to the apartment. The expression on her face at the emergence of light and the embrace of gratitude with tears in her eyes moved me also to tears. How was it possible that a person could live in extreme conditions of low support and ignorance just five blocks from the state capitol? The story of the light bulb made the rounds of the community and soon we were able to offer other modes of assistance that once appeared unreachable or far too complex. Every week we used one of the church buses to take people shopping at a farmer's market were supply and prices were significantly more affordable. Programs of house repair were accelerated with provision of leftover materials by builders and construction groups. A general clean up of yards gave the neighborhood a fresh look and retired teachers volunteered to provide after-school enrichment in the elementary school. Eventually the enrichment was expanded in a local church to include middle and high school students that eventually gained scholarships in local universities. Not all ideas came from me but the trust of the community had been vested on me and I then became a catalyst for other ideas. All things were possible. The walls in my office hold plaques and certificates of appreciation but nothing is better than the light in my heart that burns like a prayer of thanks for the gifts and talents God had vested upon me to make this effort worthwhile. During five years I was able to see the Promised Land that could be made possible by the faithful under the power of the Spirit if we only had the courage to do rather than merely watch and wish.

Seminary work took portions of one full day a week with travel to the main campus for a week of classes every three months. Testing was done often and homework flowed with abundance. Travel to New Orleans was a drive of about 7 hours that appeared to be less with the expectation of class content feeding the commitment. Saturday mornings came into play when more time for languages was needed. Somehow learning Biblical Hebrew became kind of a Sabbath exercise under the guidance of a very kind old scholar. Not all seminarians took languages since their main concern was the study of Scripture outlines solely for preaching purposes. They saw the sermon as the central park of the worship assembly and focused on sermons outlines for each bible text. There was no thought in me of becoming a preacher to lead a church and advance in the denominational rankings. I was interested in knowing Scripture and building a structure of support for social action. The seminary work was not quite as exhausting as my undergraduate journey but nonetheless demanding, especially the sojourns at the main campus that involved not only the long drive but also a parenthesis on other activities. I was the odd older professional rather than the youth minister or part time pastor seeking validation of a calling. A calling that often called for wives to have a parallel job to support ministry while the husband held part time work that permitted full time ministry. Somehow, they came to estimate that this sacrifice would be rewarded at some point with a larger congregation and a consequent better remuneration outcome. My desire was not along those lines since it had been engraved in my mind that I would be the provider for my family and God had gifted me with great amounts of talent and skill to make that provision. We worked as a family blending in love the provision God had made. In this manner, professional and pro-bono work forced some long evenings and a need for increased efficiency along with more focused prayer. Merton kept coming to mind with his call to unity: *"If you want a spiritual life you must unify your life"* (*Thoughts on Solitude.* Abbey of our Lady of Gethsemani. 1956). Somehow I had a tiger by the tail while juggling several balls with my feet. Sort of the quandary of Baloo the bear in "The Jungle Book" as he struggled with Shere Khan the Bengal tiger. Could it be that my middle age created an unnecessary sense of urgency? How far and how fast should I go? What was the timetable?

Memorized Scripture came alive for me and a search for Jesus began to take greater emphasis in life and actions. It was not so much a pursuit of sainthood but rather a search for the holy. I wanted a dialogue with God rather than a whining exercise. Seminary equipped me with some measure of order in theological thinking that now ran along the intensity of labor in all fronts. Life was being united to a spiritual pursuit not yet fully comprehended. Memory and study promoted a symbiosis that enhanced work and life. I was becoming something yet unknown but pleasing to experience. Again, Merton came to mind: *"We find God in our own being which is the mirror of God."* (*Thoughts in Solitude*). It was evident some work was taking place in me somewhat beyond my awareness but close to my delight.

All in all, graduation from the seminary came as a welcome relief while work in the neighborhood began to produce some fruits with house repairs, new construction and several initiatives in education and leadership. My church engaged with local small churches to promote spiritual development and community action. Vacant land was transformed into affordable townhouses and a neighborhood scheduled to become a parking lot became instead a revitalized small town. In the midst of all I was ordained as a minister in the Southern Baptist Church as I had now become deeply immersed in the issue of poverty and its solution. The much sought after quiet times of contemplation had given way to a cacophony of need. It was necessary to remain calm in the midst of strife and confusion. The labor of six years stood then without personal attribution as testimony of the power of the Spirit. I was exhausted but content in the realization of Galatians 2:20[4] that had been one of the first verses prescribed for my memory by the old pastor that had mentored me a few years back. Certainly, he would be smiling from above. I had kept the faith and taken some firm steps in my journey taking my mind and my heart along.

There is always a bend coming up on any path. We might expect it but do not know what comes with it. The Abbey of Gethsemani defines itself by quoting Merton's suggestion that we must *entertain silence in the heart and listen for the voice of God – to pray for your own discovery* This can apply as well to life in general rather than merely to the spiritual life. My own discovery at this time was more about silence than listening. Federico Fellini, the Italian movie director, once stated that *when you pull a little tail do not be surprised to find an elephant at the end of it*. So it was with me. I had been enlarged from the young high school student confronting the conflict of society into a trained professional confronting the same problems with more lucidity and skills. Despite it all, lots of noise still surrounded me and Gethsemani appeared once again as the model of a good destination of mind and heart to muffle the sound. The realization of a wish or completion of a task is frightening and induces a desire to escape. In a fallen world we often fail to understand the consequences of our beneficence. The escape to solitude is presented as a tempting solution; however, there is no safe way to unplug without bringing in unwelcome darkness. Still, there had to be a way to safely build a Gethsemani refuge in the midst of busy life intersections rather than merely playing in traffic wishing to be alone. Certainly, silence was the great clarifying and calming element that

---

[4] *"I have been crucified with Christ and it is no longer I who live, but Christ who lives in me. And the life that I live in the flesh I live by faith in the Son of God who loved me and gave himself for me"* ESV

could support a more focused spiritual journey as attested by the desert fathers but we had been sent to proclaim the kingdom to those places filled with people in need rather than the echo of ourselves in a cave. For me, a life in the retreat of a cloister was neither attainable nor possible but some retreating space could be built in the midst of confusion. Of course, this was harder to obtain now as on previous occasions despite the trove of memorized Scripture held in mind and being. There was still a dichotomy between physical and spiritual pursuits that created confusion and pain along with great tension. Somehow, there was a need to unify. The path was neither straight nor flat and the noise had multiple decibel levels seeking harmony. It would be best to bear all things in the hope of reaching calmer regions. Bearing upon prayer and contemplation focused upon Jesus. In this I often supplemented meditation with the advice in the hymn: *"Take Time to be Holy"*[5] (William D. Longstaff) that I had sung several times with great devotion during worship services and resounded in my mind quite often at these times. By no means had I obtained a high level of bliss but now I knew what was needed.

In the middle of the exultation that life was becoming, my father-in-law passed away from organ failure and we were forced into an examination of the meaning and extent of the commandment to honor father and mother. How far and for how long? We were called then to look beyond the bend on the road and discover a fresh new emphasis for the journey with the assurance of unknown blessings. To enjoy the certainty

---

[5] *Take time to be holy, speak oft with thy Lord; Abide in Him always, and feed on His Word. Make friends of God's children, help those who are weak, Forgetting in nothing His blessing to seek.*

Take time to be holy, the world rushes on; Spend much time in secret, with Jesus alone. By looking to Jesus, like Him thou shalt be; Thy friends in thy conduct His likeness shall see.

Take time to be holy, let Him be thy Guide; And run not before Him, whatever betide. In joy or in sorrow, still follow the Lord, And, looking to Jesus, still trust in His Word.

Take time to be holy, be calm in thy soul, Each thought and each motive beneath His control. Thus led by His Spirit to fountains of love, Thou soon shalt be fitted for service above

of *"things unseen"* as a matter of faith[6] as posited in the book of *Hebrews*. Caring for a widowed mother called for a new question: Was it sufficient to merely keep in touch by letter and telephone or was it necessary to attend personally in view of the needs of a person now advanced in years? We began by travelling often across 4 states to spend some time but soon this was not enough. Arrivals and departures caused conflicts of all sorts. Thus, we decided to move and share a home with her rather than bringing her to live with us and avoid the impact that such a radical move would cause in her wellbeing. As the only child, my wife felt a great burden for the care of her mother and being close to family. This was for us both a source of joy and trepidation. Living away from extended family had given us a strong sense of independence with little need for compromises and visitations.

From simple exegesis it is possible to understand that *"To honor"* entails a large diversity of things regardless of distances and obstacles in both language and life. It demands some level of sacrifice as all the commandments do. It is all a matter of giving rather than merely taking. The Hebrew is *ha-dar* that relates to the majesty of God, His magnificence. This equates in some way the father and the mother with the paternal presence and creative reality of God himself. In a way "to honor" is akin to worship or revere. Not that parents are divinities per se but that they represent the divine, the holy presence. The gospels (Luke2: 51) testify of Jesus obedience (honor) to his human parents as well as to his heavenly father.

The move also had additional benefits like having the grandson available at all times and connecting with the extended family for the sake of context. This type of family reunification could be the source

---

[6] *"Now faith is the assurance of things hoped for, the conviction of things not seen"*. Hebrews 11:1–ESV

of many blessings rather than conflicts. Just like repairing a community, the reunification of family also answered to the purposes of God. Whole families support wholeness of community and church. We then made a plan to cancel all professional debts and obligations while setting a date certain for moving. My business activities could continue in the new location unburdened by local financial and professional entanglements. This was not so much a leap but rather a triple somersault of faith. Much to our surprise, we nailed the landing without breaking our necks either physically or spiritually. Prayers spoken and unspoken had been answered, everybody was accommodated in the new home and a local university offered me a tenure track position that reduced the pressure to do business in uncertain and likely less auspicious conditions. In none of my dreams had this scenario been possible.

Contrary to our previous move, we had not made an extensive search for a church home and decided to attend the one her mother was attending for the sake of her convenience since we had to provide for her transportation. It was a United Methodist congregation with long acquaintances both to my wife and her mother. The pastor had performed our wedding ceremony. Despite our best efforts, our evangelical norms did not fit well in the life and spirit of the congregation. Our emphasis on Bible study was in contrast with the discussion of social justice issues professed by the leadership yet we stayed on waiting for some form of spiritual content for our journey akin to the one promoted by John Wesley more than 200 years in the past. Like the protagonists of the Samuel Beckett play *"Waiting for Godot"* we waited in vain. In all, we found the spiritual climate rather stunted and the theology quite loose and easy despite the enthusiasm of the membership. The intensity of the Great Awakening had long ceased. In this place at this time the processes of spiritual discovery encouraged by Merton and others had stalled and become unchallenging. There was no discernable fire other than social engagement. Most certainly, we were quite removed from John Wesley and the Great Awakening by more than time and location.

Thus, we decided to follow an invitation to join a Presbyterian Church in America congregation a few blocks away. By then we were cautious but hopeful. We needed a church home for worship and instruction without the need for a long commute. This was most likely a great choice from all appearances. Good teaching, good preaching, good environment of community. We had arrived at the moment when study of the *Westminster Confession* was under way. It was a well-articulated presentation over several weeks that gladdened our hearts thirsty for a semblance of instruction. It all made sense except for a few lawyerly issues of election and salvation that we thought could be overcome or tolerated for the sake of community. Despite this I was invited to teach in Sunday school and accepted the call to conduct a study of *"Exodus"* as one of the approved Sunday classes. There was great interest from the 20 or so students and class preparation brought out not only exegetical and hermeneutical skills but also a wonderful awakening of spiritual life by way of a deeper immersion in Scripture. Those Saturdays at seminary studying Biblical Hebrew were coming in handy. I could deliver meaning and clarity with opportune insight. My teaching skills were no longer dormant in the pew and exploded with enthusiasm as they had in the academic classroom. Somehow the heritage of my father and an aunt as teachers fed me in this time of great self-realization about a gift of teaching that had been kept well hidden within me. However, the need for silence to hear God became progressively stronger the more I studied for the class purposes. The resulting tension was quite strong as I struggled with issues of pride in the teaching work and a balance with humility on the spiritual walk. Certainly one cannot be proud of being humble.

The congregation had a well-established custom of socialization before and after worship services that was quite often distracting. My view of the sanctuary as a quiet place of veneration and contemplation ran counter to the reality of a social encounter. This was further complicated by the selection of music at worship. For some reason, the pastor believed in promoting the endless singing of well meaning spiritual ditties accompanied by tambourine shaking and guitar riffs. These introductory exercises akin to muscular warm-ups failed to elevate my spirit to the intended heights. There had to be another way to worship and gain space for contemplation. God was not expecting spiritual aerobic exercises but rather to be still and know that he was God (Psalm 46:10). It was quite simply a stratagem to create excitement with a veneer of spirituality. A man made device that somehow negated the power of the Spirit to instruct and to guide very reminiscent of the parable of the Pharisee and the tax collector praying at the temple (Luke 18:9-14). God responds to a search in silence rather than in ostentatious displays of noisemaking regardless of piety of feelings or goodness of intentions. Micah had addressed this in summary: *What does the LORD require of you but to do justice, and to love kindness, and to walk humbly with your God?* (Micah 6:8). The humble walk was a silent connector to the voice of God. No need for electronic amplification or childish sentimentality. My search then included the earnest pursuit of silence as a means to a connection with God and His word.

Soon I decided to quit teaching and join a Lutheran congregation where my son played the organ. Listening to the organ works in the quietness of the sanctuary elevated my mind and heart toward the divine. I could see Jesus on the horizon beyond the high walls of Calvinism that had surrounded me in the Presbyterian Church. It did not matter if I could be one of the elect. That was a legalistic construct settled on a cross in Calvary rather than on Calvin's desk where my freedom from man-made shackles of faith had been gained through death and resurrection rather than a legalistic construct in Geneva. I really wanted to go back home to my roots but there was much fear to conquer. Like the prodigal son I was ready to say: *"Father, I have sinned against heaven and before you. I am no longer worthy to be called your son. Treat me as one of your hired servants."* however, the time was not ripe. I had been gone for almost 50 years and in my fearful heart there was the expectation of a painful rejection.

Thus, I committed myself to life in Lutheranism although my mind was not eager to fight in the Reformation any more. I merely wanted to have a quiet time with God in the Church of my first baptism and communion.

Five: A Clearer View

DISCIPLING INTO THE LUTHERAN CONGREGA-
tion included many conversations with the pastor and some actions of
service. There was a culture almost akin to my memory of a Catholic
church. Above all there was time for quiet contemplation in the amber
mist of a sanctuary illuminated by stained glass windows along each
aisle. Very soon I was enrolled in the usher corps to welcome worship-
pers and guide the flow of people to the communion rail. The mystery of the real presence worked joy in my heart. I was finally finding
the spiritual anchorage I had been seeking in my journey. Christ in the
Eucharist enriching and transforming my entire being as I remembered
from a youthful age.

I began then to explore the *Lectio Divina* as a means of dedicating
time for reading, meditation, prayer and contemplation in a more
organized manner. My devotional efforts since seminary had been
somewhat unbalanced and the reading of several descriptive books
on *Lectio Divina*[7] had began to expose me to a greater dimension of
engagement with the faith and God himself. I was far from becoming a

---

[7]   It had all began with Richard Foster's *Celebration of Discipline* (Harper, San Francisco. 1978)
    that opened my eyes to a personal effort to engage Scripture and Life with a framework of
    order and purpose beyond immediate satisfaction. He had followed a few years later with
    Meditative Prayer (Intervarsity, Downers Grove, 1983), which truly enriched my prayer life.
    Since I am an avid reader and researcher, my library was soon enriched with several books on
    Lectio Divina. The following is a general bibliography that attests (if anything) to a process of

monk but wanted to be close to God beyond the formalities of worship and scattered reading for exegetical purposes. The challenges posed by my teaching schedule at the university were great but somehow time became available when I least expected it. The research helped me immensely by expanding both understanding of dimension and purpose of engagement. As with all things, it took some time before I put the actual reading into practice. Once a routine was established, my soul rejoiced and the straitjacket of Calvinism acquired in the Presbyterian congregation began to loosen up and disappear. To follow a strict interpretation of the *Westminster Confession* with all its contradictions and legalistic processes had proven increasingly difficult. The shortcomings of Reformed Theology are vast regarding the extent of the atonement, the covenant of works, the doctrine of the church and the inerrancy of Scripture just to mention a few. I was neither interested nor willing to embrace Calvin or Geneva. Undoubtedly, The *Westminster Confession* it is a well written document skillfully articulated but its vision of a sovereign, angry and just God punishing sinners rather than a loving and merciful God seeking sinners stands in contrast to the work and words of Jesus: *I have come to seek and to save the lost* (Luke 19:10). He did not come to affirm the Pharisees or establish a new set of regulations.

---

searching or a type of bibliographical pilgrimage. The authors come from various Christian disciplines:

Benner, David: *Opening to God: Lectio Divina and Life as Prayer*. IVP Books, Downers Grove. 2010

Foster, Dom David: *Reading with God: Lectio Divina*. Downside Abbey, Bloomsbury-Continuum. New York/London. 2006

MacGrath, Alister: *Christian Spirituality: An Introduction*. Blackwell, Oxford. 1999

Studzinski, Dom Raymond, OSB: *Reading to Live: The Evolving Practice of Lectio Divina*. Cistercian Publications. Abbey of Gethsemani. 2010

Thompson, Marjorie: *Soul Feast: An Invitation to The Christian Spiritual Life*. Westminster John Knox Press. Louisville. 1995

Wilhoit, James: *Discovering Lectio Divina: Bringing Scripture into Ordinary Life*. IVP. Downers Grove. 2012

There is no mention of predestination anywhere in the words and work of Jesus or for that matter of a listing of the elect and the condemned. The infinite mind of Jesus does not need a list to know who is in Him. There is simply a call to repentance and righteousness in all His messages. He descended between burial and resurrection (Ephesians 4:9-10) to take captives upward rather than execute or further confine them to a lower abyss of eternal despair. In this light the Fatima Prayer: *"O my Jesus, forgive us our sins, save us from the fires of hell, and lead all souls to Heaven, especially those in most need of Your Mercy"* stands more closely to the truth than a legalistic argument handicapped by the events of a human time of conflict. The mercy of God is not restricted by human argumentation that excludes the contribution of tradition all the way to creation by a focus on the immediate around 1517.

The reading of Scripture along with Patristic Literature was reaffirming in me the continuous salvation action of a merciful God and the eternal calling of Jesus to the place he had promised to prepare. It also served to expose me more directly once again to the long history of the Catholic Church and the preservation of the faith in the face of various conflicts and attacks. I sort of had known this since elementary school and seminary days but I had ignored it for the sake of finding what I estimated would be a better and greater truth in my own way. Reading Jaroslav Pelikan across his five volumes of church history (*The Christian Tradition*, 1975-1991) and his study of the historical creeds and confessions of faith in the Christian tradition (*Credo*, 2005) served to refine my perspective and further reaffirm my longing for a return to the Catholic faith. Nonetheless, the Lutheran Church roughly approximated the Catholic Church of my childhood and I fitted comfortably in its liturgy and teachings. Soon I ended up as head usher by default after a member moved out of town and a few months later I was called to be an elder. The task was not a difficult one and was made easier by my corporate experience in running my own firm augmented by my increasing self-identity in Christ. We were then searching for a pastor and much time was spent doing evaluations of candidates. My pleasure rested in weekly communion and practice of *Lectio Divina* along with the study of Lutheran writings (*Book of Concord* etc) to gain a better understanding of this faith expression. It seemed as if time had expanded to afford me moments of reading, meditation, praying, and contemplation. My academic teaching schedule provided several moments of quiet time I came to value for meditation and contemplation. In the midst of all, two issues began to occupy my thoughts: Retirement and a long held desire to walk the Way of St. James. I began to plan for both and a sabbatical leave emerged to promote the walk and postpone the retirement for a couple of years.

With the journey on the Camino carefully planned, my wife and I set for France right after my son's wedding in mid May 2010. We intended to walk from Le Puy en Velay in the slopes of the Massif Central in southern France to Santiago de Compostela in the extreme northwest corner of Spain. It would be a journey of about 1,000 miles in 66 days across sites of the ancient church connected by a pathway where pilgrims had walked for more than 800 years. In these localities had been fought battles for truth and had been planted centers of learning and worship by various orders and rulers. We intended to arrive in Santiago on July 25 for the feast of St. James in a year of Jubilee. We made it one day in advance. The exhaustion of the walk was softened by the joy of the spirit. To this day the dimension of the effort remains ever fresh in our minds and has supported a continued journey of faith and eventual transformation. The walk on el Camino started in the mild climate of mid spring and ended in the very hot days of summer at the jubilee celebration in Santiago. Every step connected me to the root of faith in the Catholic Church. Ancient churches, sacred ruins, majestic cathedrals, small sanctuaries and memorials of faith spoke eloquently of a faith that had stood the challenges of time and man across centuries. In all; however, there remained in my heart the ever-insistent fear of divine rejection. The Calvinist punishment to be inflicted by an angry God upon a wretched sinner kept coming to mind as if thoughts of an evil condition were difficult to erase. Nevertheless, the enormity of the cathedrals in Leon, Burgos and Santiago seemed to give proof of a loving and creative Father bestowing mercy and forgiveness in His children for the single purpose of His glory. It was a welcome message carved in the architecture of stone. Whether repentant and forgiven or unrepentant and not forgiven all children of God seek to please the Father. The obedience of some is contrasted with the rebellion of others. God still loves all and extends mercy to all who seek it in honesty and truth. Through the smoke of burning incense filling the nave from the big *botafumeiro* (censer) at the cathedral in Santiago we saw rays of grace and mercy reaching down to us from the stained glass windows. The remains of St. James apostle in his sarcophagus invited our embrace and veneration. The pilgrimage had brought us closer to the true faith. Our sore legs stood as exclamation points or physical alleluias.

Upon our return we gave several chats and I wrote a couple of books related to the issue of spatial perception. What is what you see in the land? How do you understand what you see? The same questions were directed to my spiritual walk. What is it that I see in the church and the tradition? Like lava in a volcano, a premonition of great forces was working within me. When and how would I erupt? Was it a matter of my will or the will of God?

41

The exercise of *Lectio Divina* became a discipline and it framed my days while writing, teaching or doing academic research. It probably fed the lava boiling in my volcano. At no point had I become a Benedictine monk but was instead a calm and focused student of Scripture enlarging content, context and meaning while pushing me away from the strictures of Reform Theology. There was no need to argue with Calvin or check my standing on the list of the elect. I had opted out as quietly as when I had arrived. The true faith beckoned. The time had come to answer the call.

Following upon the legacy of the effort in Atlanta, I began to promote a similar enterprise around the Lutheran church that was now my spiritual home. It was a simpler matter of rehabilitation of homes, construction of a few infill units, paving of sidewalks and providing incentives for young families to repopulate the area. This could be used as a model for other areas that once housed students but had now lost attractiveness to young people by reason of more modern apartment complexes. The church owned several of these homes and the idea of a small town around a church seemed like a good idea. Unfortunately, my proposal was rejected in favor of a one day hand out of canned goods and second hand winter coats that engaged a portion of the membership in what was seen as short and quick action of mercy.

My experience with the timidity of church organizations made the rejection palatable and enabled the continuation of work with my students on community revitalization projects that feed the long held expectations of various organizations and community associations across the state. With the intention of instilling a social consciousness to their eventual professional work my students enthusiastically engaged in the production of concepts for recovery and organization of communities. Each academic year we did one or two of these projects with well received products presented in booklet and video formats that remained as tools and inspiration for each community. Many development plans came out of these concepts and ideas and many students have gone on to promote these types of efforts in their practices. These young men are church members in various denominations and locations. Their ethical formation is likely to influence their places of work as well as those of worship. The notion that skills are a divine gift as patrimony for the benefit of community is deeply held in Catholic ethical thought and affirmed in a large number of encyclicals and documents that celebrate human environment and habitation. Thus, the solution to the poverty problem resides more in the creation of better human environment rather than in food and goods distribution. Provision of food is important but the creation of safe, humane and appropriate housing is critical to elevate people above mere subsistence. This is not an entirely Catholic issue but rather a spiritual response that might incidentally lead others to the faith but serves nonetheless to heal the barren places and the people living in them. Some portion of the redemptive work of God might well be assigned outside the boundaries and processes of the Catholic Church despite protestations to the contrary.

Six: The Eagle Returns to the Launching Pad

WHEN JOHN F. KENNEDY PROPOSED SENDING A man to the moon and returning him safely to earth he might well be describing a journey of discovery for many faithful. Getting to the moon was relatively easy. Getting back to the earth implied problems of re-entry and landing. How to prevent burning in the atmosphere? How to regulate the speed of entry and the safety of the splashdown? The physics alone for the entire operation were dauntingly complex. The Apollo capsule was really akin to a meteorite entering the atmosphere. Its design and travel path needed to protect human life rather than behaving as a mere metal box dropping to earth. Much research and experimentation was done in metallurgy and avionics at high temperatures and speeds to reach certainty that a re-entry was safe and possible. In a similar way and in His mercy, God had prepared a re-entry vehicle for His lost sheep. Would I be ready to enter it? Could I summon the courage to trust the Supreme designer?

Three years after the walk to Santiago the time came for retirement after completing the writing of a couple of books and selling a great portion of my personal library for the benefit of the student association. It was all very pleasant but still life altering. My son and his young family had been just two hours away and we could visit often. Then, he was called to a job farther south and we found ourselves facing a drive of about 15 hours to visit with them. We took an initial trip to accompany them in house searching at their new location. It became a two-day driving excursion each way since I could no longer exert energy on a fast one day drive. Somehow one begins to recognize that the Second Law of Thermodynamics affects you as much as other natural laws. I was no longer the young man who could drive forever. My eyes and my back took turns arguing for their comfort. After all the years, they finally had their way. Upon our return from the exploration trip and in consideration of the nature of the travel effort we decided to move south in order to be close to my son and his family.

Retirement is something you can do anywhere. There are neither schedules nor limits other than self-imposed ones. However, moving called for untangling from possessions, relationships and acquaintances. The comfort of the daily and usual would be shattered. Our new living quarters were to be vastly smaller than the current ones. The arrangement would be much in the manner of the home where I grew up with grandparents and aunts all around. In this new location we would have a large bedroom, a bath, and a room for my office at one end of the house while sharing the rest for different needs and functions. There would certainly be a need for accommodation and communion. Our large house of 3,000 square feet had to be condensed to fit in about 800 square feet. Gone also was a perennial garden that after 10 years had began to bloom as planned and planted. Friends and places that had framed our lives for 16 years were now to become distant points in the rearview mirror. The familiar was being transferred to the unfamiliar. But we had done it before.

God was preparing a new path for our journey. In using "our" I am reflecting the nature of marriage. It is no longer I and she or myself and herself. My wife and I are cleaved to one another and we are no longer two separate, independent entities. She has accompanied my walk and to a large extent it is also her walk. Most certainly, we will have responsibility for individual actions and choices but in all we march as one.

This also reminds me of Christ in a reality beyond mere evangelical appropriation when we say to be one in with him as a play pal for the moment of a sentimental song but rather on a deeper view and understanding of Him being in us to save and to rule. It is an issue of dimension. The later involves feelings of the moment while the former implies submission of the will across eternity. The search for Christ becomes the total measure of life rather than a mere devotional activity. Believing is one thing and being transformed is another. Of course, this is a point of discussion that can take time and falls somewhat outside the scope of this story. I try very hard to avoid theological discussions that are speculative in nature and tone. The point is that evangelicals by focusing solely on a worship of Christ alone seem to ignore the wider perspective of the faith anchored in Scripture and sustained in tradition across history. A larger union that is part of a much larger stature rather than a mere personal pocket size devotional intent. The perception of something larger that connects us to the entire measure of creation (Ephesians 4:4-6 and 4:13)[8] is lacking by the elimination of history and tradition.

We all have a traceable ancestry and faith is no exception. It all began at a point much before 1517 and has continued through the ages to this day. Christ has been in it ever since and before as a protagonist rather than as a mere spectator. Perhaps by capturing Christ solely for us we take Him out of the grand stage of salvation history and confine Him

---

[8] *There is one body and one Spirit, just as you were called to one hope when you were called; one Lord, one faith, one baptism; one God and Father of all, who is over all and through all and in all....(Eph 4:4-6) Until we all reach unity in the faith and in the knowledge of the Son of God, as we mature to the full measure of the stature of Christ. (Eph 4:13)*

to our sanctuaries bereft of context or significance. The five *solas* of the Reformation seem to shrink the playing field into a circular small pitch of momentary significance with closely cropped grass surface suitable only for a friendly game of croquet or marbles rather than a hard game of football or soccer in context with the richness of Nature all around. The Roman Catholic Church of the 14th and 15th century no longer exists as much as Calvin's church in Geneva and other Protestant congregations of the time have faded into history. The Reformation fulfilled a mission in its time and contrary to the wishes of its leader became a religious organization with the same complexity as the projected reform he had proposed. Like all organizations started by humans it eventually reaches entropy and perishes without a connection to an eternal legacy able to project it across time. It becomes then a mere black hole in space. Tradition seems to support a genetic reason for being that extends before and after us very much in the manner of a spiritual DNA reaching across centuries to prove ancestry. We are sons of God beyond and before our faith decision if we understand that all is well established before and after us within a divine plan[9] as stated by Scripture and the prophets. In the meaning of the word "prophet" we are related indeed as "spokesmen" for the work of grace rather than church members with afflictions and anguished needs for consolation. It is the prophetic calling that empowers the Church for action rather than a mere place to get out of the rain or the sun. Jesus dedicated (ordained or made holy) us to be his witnesses (prophets) everywhere (Act 1:8) imbued by the Holy Spirit. There is no other greater challenge. Of course there is the calling of believers as saints by St. Paul rather than mere faithful. It was a way to denote our holiness (hagios) or dedication to the purposes

---

[9] *"Before I formed you in the womb I knew you, and before you were born I consecrated you; I appointed you a prophet to the nations."* Jeremiah 1:5

of creation more than membership in the volumes of the canonized. Paul refers to believers as saints in Romans 16:2, Ephesians 4:12 and again in Ephesians 5:3. In all, Paul refers to the saints about 67 times in his letters to express a level of tenderness for the believers who were taking their baby steps in the faith. Saint meant then the imitators of Christ who by their baptism were declared holy and sanctified or saints. The Roman Catholic Church eventually chose to refer as "saint" only to those in heaven duly canonized while Scripture calls "saint" those on earth living out their faith with fear and trembling. We will find out that is what on the last day and thereafter. My ambition is not to reach canonization but rather to look at myself in the mirror and see the face of Christ. I never ceased to believe yet was not believing in the church of my baptism. Somehow I had found a better fit along a Protestant viewpoint although not entirely confident with the entirety of the Protestant position. I now return to the faith as a believer rather than a theologian.

Once settled in our new home we began attending Sunday mass finding delight in the liturgy and the spiritual climate around us. We were crossing a bridge by faith not unlike Indiana Jones in his quest for the Holy Grail. The environment was not physically different from the Lutheran sanctuary but there was the feeling that the place was full of the timeless presence of the saints. There was a greater context unseen but palpable. There were long antecedents to our presence that provided comfort and assurance. We were truly surrounded by many witnesses that dated from centuries before 1517. The focus of the mass upon the Eucharist rather than the homily was noteworthy. We wanted very much to take communion but were yet unable. My wife had been a protestant all her life and I had marched away from the church for 56 years into various shades of Protestantism. We needed to make things right, to take the right steps. The five steps of the examination (examen)

49

defined by Loyola have been merging across my life into a final single approach lane. The space capsule had entered the atmosphere. This was the true way of Christ.

Pope Francis had decreed a Year of Mercy in 2016 in his bull *"Misericordiae Vultus"* along with the constant call for Catholics to come home. We wrapped our hope in it and were standing at the gate ready to enter and return. Our inquiry led us to be enrolled in RCIA classes to begin looking forward to the Vigil of Easter and then the formal acceptance into the church. As a cradle Catholic all I had to do was to seek reconciliation through confession but I waited for my wife to complete the instruction as a means of encouragement as well as a refresher of sorts. One critical step was the convalidation of our marriage under Catholic law. We had been doing all things together and this step had to be done as one in seeking the sacramental blessing of the church.

The weeks in RCIA enabled me to reconnect more effectively with the faith and dissipate doubts and apprehensions. Beyond theology there was a sense of discovery as Merton had indicated. Finding my spiritual self on a proper foundation was exciting. The exercise in *Lectio Divina* gave way to a daily reading of the *Liturgy of the Hours*[10] that falls along the same lines but offers a more structured discipline of study, prayer and meditation. It makes one more aware of time in a format that soon becomes natural and quite easy to follow for someone in his retirement years. As a complement I followed the daily mass office in the *Daily Roman Missal*[11] *with* occasional watching of the mass at EWTN. Going back to my Father's house was just a matter of time and forgiveness as well as dedication. There was work to be done by the prodigal son after the reception banquet. It was not so much a matter of recovering

---

[10] *The Liturgy of the Hours*. Catholic Publishing Corporation. New York. 1975

[11] *Daily Roman Missal*. Midwest Theological Forum, Inc. Woodridge, IL. 2012

proximity but rather an issue of rejoicing in time. There are no clocks in eternity. My soul was excited at the return journey and I could see now that all stations on the journey had offered some formative value. I had found not just Jesus but Christ, a brother and redeemer.

Much had changed in the church since Vatican II and I took time to read the conciliar and post-conciliar documents[12] while conquering the fears (probably embarrassment) of a return in my late age that reminded me of Ignatius of Loyola studying Latin with school children. Often our sense of human propriety prevents the honest expression of our sentiments or ignorance. More often it is a matter of the desire to be considered duly informed and wise. It is a conflict of the mind rather than the spirit that imbues our honest response to issues and circumstances very much like the verses of the old tango *Volver* (To Return) [13] that expresses in a non-liturgical way the emotion of going back home after a lifelong absence with the trepidation of arriving and not knowing what type of welcome to expect. Certainly, there are psalms and pieces of Scripture that describe a return in better theological terms but a tango does it for me. It is part of what I have been and somehow describes well the emotion of ending a journey at the autumn of life toward a place of origin.

---

[12] Flannery, Austin OP, General Editor: *Vatican Council II: The Conciliar and Post- Conciliar Documents*. Liturgical Press, Collegeville, MN. 1996

[13] *I imagine the flickering*
of the lights that in the distance
will be marking my return.
They're the same that lit,
with their pale reflections,
deep hours of pain
And even though I didn't want to come back,
you always return to your first love
The tranquil street where the echo said
yours is her life, yours is her love,
under the mocking gaze of the stars
that, with indifference, today see me return.

Volver. Lyrics by Carlos Gardel and Alfredo Lepera, 1930

Every time I went home to visit my family there was a heightened expectation of seeing the old places and reinforcing memories. Moreover, there was in all the fear of disconnection. Of having lost fluency in the vernacular language of family, friends and place. So it is with a return to the foundational stock of the faith. Does the grafting still hold? It is hard to forget origins, to eliminate memories and comfortable relationships. I had been grafted not only into the faith but also into family and community from my earliest age. My life abroad in a different culture only served to enlarge all that I could be and do. A fusion of cultures had occurred in me that enabled transit between cultures and promoted changes of benefit to me as well as my family. More than a refugee I was a prophet or spokesman for two cultures and one faith. In this light, Ephesians 4: 1-6 acquired new meaning beyond what I had memorized some years back: *I therefore, a prisoner for the Lord, urge you to walk in a manner worthy of the calling to which you have been called, with all humility and gentleness, with patience, bearing with one another in love, eager to maintain the unity of the Spirit in the bond of peace. There is one body and one Spirit—just as you were called to the one hope that belongs to your call— one Lord, one faith, one baptism, one God and Father of all, who is over all and through all and in all.* Most certainly the church was calling through the Spirit for a return to the one body in truth. The calling had not been cancelled. The journey had not been in vain but there was now a place of arrival.

Witnessing the instruction of RCIA brought back memories of childhood and youth at church. Memories of catechism instruction, hymns, prayers and events came to the forefront to promote the expectation of a reunion of sorts with family and place. There was no need to fight in the Reformation army any longer. I was now being reformed by the Holy Spirit some 2,100 miles away from the place where I was first formed as a Christian. Perhaps this was a rebirth or a fresh baptism. Kind of a response to the call of John the Baptist on the shores of the Jordan. A call to a river of forgiveness (Reorientation? Redirection?) that runs out of the land of Mannaseh not just into the Dead Sea but flows figuratively everywhere to nurture our life of faith wherever we can be. I had been baptized soon after birth in a Catholic church and had been baptized again as an adult in Community and Baptist churches. Somehow there has been a washing and an initiation of sorts across stages of my life. Yet, it seemed as if all had been a journey on a Mobius strip. A journey of eternal dimensions on the same surface for the single purpose of finding the face of Christ in the mirror. That moment under the water, shortly after birth inscribed in me a destiny that challenged a return and a fresh commitment. Sort of a watermark inscribed upon my soul by the Maker of the folio of life and destiny. A sign of provenance, ownership and artisanship that placed me in His flock. We had been made for Jesus and belonged to Him for all eternity (John 10:28-30). Thus, my first confession after 50 plus years was more than a mere act of contrition. It was a celebration of return. A much welcomed arrival to a place of rest and the fuller realization of myself. After all, Merton was right. I had to encounter my true self.

The Vigil of Easter and all the accompanying rites and celebrations brought much happiness to my wife who had made her first confession and communion. We both shared the moment of receiving the Eucharist somewhat overwhelmed by the dimension of the faith and the mercy of God that connected us to the long tradition and life of the church as well as the pathway to eternity. We were dimensionally larger in the spirit than ever and humanly happier than ever. There could not have been a more joyous moment.

After Easter Sunday our devotional life merged on one accord fed by her discovery of the lives of saints (Martin, James, SJ. *My Life with the Saints.* Loyola Press, Chicago. 2006) and their example for personal life action. Her enthusiasm, devotion and piety are remarkable and encourage a similar response on my side. This is truly the best experience of our lives. The best illustration of cleaving unto one another.

Thus I sit now as an old pilgrim on the figurative veranda of the true church watching the narrative of life flowing before my eyes. In many ways it is reminiscent of the times we had at the end of each stage on the Way of Saint James. Doing each day a meditation and contemplation of the journey and looking forward to the next stage. Most certainly, I am not so much a saint as someone sanctified by the power of the Spirit and the experience of the absence and the search. As always, Merton walks in with some words of commentary and encouragement: *"For me to be a saint means to be myself. Therefore the problem of sanctity and salvation is in fact the problem of finding out who I am and rediscovering my true self" New Seeds of Contemplation.* New Directions. New York. 1961) But it was not sainthood and salvation that I was pursuing insofar as I have been more of an aint than a saint. My goal was Christ and the impact of his power to provide a solution to poverty. Now I know that there is no solution in as much as our mortal flesh and its limitations alongside the rule of Satan in the world encumber us. Our damnation is also the damnation of the poor. The solution to poverty resides entirely upon the riches in glory in the routing we are able to map out for others with our faith. Through the journey I have become myself and now live comfortably in my skin within the silence that Christ provides. Silence that enables action in faith and a better listening to the Word of God. My journey exhausted my commitment for human action and left me alone with the precious silence of meditation where Christ comes near to redeem rather than condemn.

There is in all the satisfaction of having become a servant to communities and people with the holy purpose of achieving a fuller life with the generous use of talents and skills. Action with a congregation might have proven difficult but the work of my students across 16 years has been redemptive far beyond expectations. The world is changed with courage and imagination taken into action rather than merely containing them in procedures and formulations. This seems to explain the walk of Jesus as well as the walk in the Camino. We all need to take steps that connect and deliver good news. So now I sit at the end of the journey sounding not so much a cry of defeat but a song of triumph made possible by Christ alone in the context of His church. As St. Paul intimates to Timothy: *"for I know whom I have believed, and I am convinced that he is able to guard until that day what has been entrusted to me"*. There was no the possibility of retreat in a convent for me but there has been a full life with all its limitations that now is re-grafted to the stock of faith and rejoices in the fresh flow of spiritual sap that now flows under my physical and spiritual skin. The ethical foundation grafted into my students will endure.

So, after a long journey of return or regress what remains? What is a prodigal pilgrim called to do? For many reasons I might be now spent and of little service. At 71 years of age my skills have eroded and the Biblical languages have slowly faded away from my memory. My theological formation really matters very little now but it was not done in vain and might yet produce more fruit. All seeds germinate in their time as provided by the Creator. Most certainly the vigor of youth is gone and has been replaced by some form of quiet wisdom or experience. In all, I am sustained by the power of the Spirit in the assurance that the plan of God for my life will be done for as long as He gives me life. In our wedding bands we have engraved a Latin phrase: *"Quoad ambi vivemus et ultra"* which means *"For as long as we both shall live and beyond"*. It is an expression of affection for a very special person along with a promise done in hope as a commitment beyond us. God will dispose in His supreme will and I will obey his disposition. We live in His time. The goal of the journey was not to capture Christ but rather to be captured by Him. Amen.

Let us therefore approach the throne of grace with boldness, so that we may receive mercy and find grace to help in time of need. Hebrews 4:16 RSV

CPSIA information can be obtained
at www.ICGtesting.com
Printed in the USA
LVHW090024120122
708364LV00005B/175